Steps

Steps

Mark Goodwin

Longbarrow Press

Published in 2014 by
Longbarrow Press
76 Holme Lane
Sheffield
S6 4JW

www.longbarrowpress.com

Printed by T.J. International Ltd,
Padstow, Cornwall

Some of these poems, or versions of, or parts of,
have been previously published in the following magazines
and books, to whose editors I am grateful:
Alpinist; *Bosigran and the North Coast*
(climbers club guides to West Cornwall, 2015);
Climber; *The Clearing*; *Fire*; *The Footing*
(anthology, Longbarrow Press, 2013);
Gists and Piths; *Hearing Voices*; *Litter Magazine*;
The Peak – Past and Present (Constable, 1998);
Poetry Salzburg; *Shearsman Magazine*;
Staffordshire Grit –The Roaches (rock-climbing guide book,
The British Mountaineering Council, 2005);
Staple; *Texts' Bones.*

ISBN 978-1-906175-24-5

First edition

and step in time to flow

vibrant meat-encased bone over

soil & stone. Without knowing

know

Walk

Put
a foot on a rock. Choose

one route through millions of pebbles. Follow
clearly seen, sometimes pain-filled paths, or abandon
people's spoor & artefact. Wander. Smell

peats' waters. Sniff

dry limestone's,
     rhyolite's, granite's, or grit's
                              dusts as ground's scuffed. Inhale

subtle or pungent sap sprays as plants are squeezed. Flex

leg-flesh. Side-step. Skip. Scamper. Mould
rough world through soles. Drum

never-the-same rhythms of picking places to balance
on along shattered ridges. Kick

into cold; wade

water's white crystal form, or through see-
                                                  through rivers. Leap
from friction-patch to
              friction-patch amongst algae-coated boulders rounded

by mountains' blood. Step

Contents

For Tess & Louis

The blue mountains are constantly walking.
If you doubt mountains walking you do not know
your own walking.

Whilst Carrying You Across Cadair Idris

For Tess

I look back,

from the top of Cyfrwy ridge,
across a sunlit cwm to where
Cadair's moss band casts

its slanting track of chlorophyll force across
the unknowingness
of rock. Alive glow. Whilst the white

trig' point gleams

its *man-made* map-maker message; tugs
            as a hub spokes
of cartographic heart strings. We've been

                                                            across

to that high point; you stowed

just behind my head; your
small exploring hands grasp,
like clinging stars, the skin
of my shoulders – the same flesh

we're both drawn from. I turn

from a view

of emerald cells mapped
across crag. I can smell

the soft oils from your baby hair swirl

in the breeze as *we* walk

(you on my back), back
from the cwm's rim,

across   rocks.

1998

Llŷn in the Moelwyns

Heather is beaded
with condensed mist.
'Not a puff of wind.'
Sunshine slides
through the mist – sprays
light.

As we wade
in heather our knees're soaked
cool. Our expressions fixed

we aim
for certainty: We read
ground through
fine detail printed
on paper; we count
our paces along
compass bearings from
this knoll to that
contour re-entrant, now
to the stream heard
trickling before it's
seen. The stream's

handrail will lead
to the llyn's bowl balanced
above us.

Dark juniper bushes push
through the mist's
brightness as we gain
height.

Our voices
are close; completely
echoless – muffled
as if indoors.

We're between
four walls of mist.

Our gaitered boots, sucked
by soaked mosses, release
with each step whiffs
of bog plants & peat. Suddenly

            the mist lifts.

The llyn's still sheet is revealed.

Cnicht's crisp ridge
            is perfectly reflected. Distance,

open air, flashes
                        of blue sky,
            greens vibrant
                                in broad light.

The llyn's banks
are short, steep crags flecked
with quartz – they form
a cove. The rock's roughness

                        & the llyn's sheen

abrade and soothe
as we scramble
round the rim.

Mist tumbles

up from the valley over

the lip

of the llyn's bowl; rolls

across its glaze towards

llên

us. We freeze. Stare. Air

llen

skims

our faces with its cool vapour

Craft

Pull
up on jugs of gritstone. Crimp
on folds of compressed sand. File
movement smooth in mind. Touch

rough quartz studs. Fashion
delicate pain in ornate thoughts. Jam
soft flesh fists tight in cracks. Sculpt
in the medium of wind-carved flakes & overlaps. Balance

desires on sharp arêtes. Chisel
excess ages away as dust. Brush
now's stone powder to heart. Breathe

viscous patterns of smell. Varnish
this shape of flesh-&-grit with sweat.   Then abandon

the creation at its top. Give
the grit-hard-&-ego-soft art up. Jump.

Or coil
up the well furred rope. Shove
its complex coloured smile into a worn rucksack.   Walk

back home slowly. Feel
arrogant and vulnerable.

ማስተከል

mastekel – verb, to plant
or to pitch

፩

we camp in Abyssinian mountains
we sleep on African ground

I fatten on African dreams
fatten on Amharic's rhythms

our tent is a pod of human seeds
a tabarnacle around life's glow

፪

Africa is hungry
she would be glad of my meat
my death would be a simple event
she would spread me on the red ground
that grew the Amharic tongue
she would pick at my stark syllables
she would leave my bones
as stony words to whiten under sun

፫

we camp in Abyssinia
we sleep on Africa

and in the soil of sleep are us seeds
and in this sleep I see

Ethiopians balance their smiles
on their teeth

፬

I cry into a bowl of soup
my spoon a huge silver tear
I cry because I am tired
because I have walked too many miles
on African ground
I cry because of teeth & Ethiopians' smiles
I cry into my bowl of soup
I cry because of warm good food
sobs round & silver as spoons burst
from the seed-pod of me

I am so weak
but strong enough to lift my spoon to eat
I have enough carbohydrate in my blood
I have enough energy to weep

I have fattened on African dreams

፭

my imagination is a fine silver trickle of water

vanishing

through the ground's deep red dust
on which the bones of my words whiten

፪

my hands are dirty with this land
my fingerprints are dark engravings

on my pale skin
she has touched me

I am engraved with Amharic ground
and yet it only takes

a shower & soap to wash Africa away
to let me slip free

to let me drain of African dreams

I watch my imagination swirl
with my dirt down a plughole

my seed bursts hollow

my thin sick imagination is lit
only by the sun's setting to the west
I am a silhouette

my knowledge a skeleton

February 2005

Beings Along the Simien Escarpment

፩

I am on the escarpment's edge   below me a solidified sea
of earth & rock waves rolls away into haze   and I am standing
on the crest of its biggest wave   a motionless tsunami   the cliff falls

directly for 300 metres and then slopes steeply for 2000 more
into the valleys below   I am balanced   on the edge of a vast tooth
and the sky is smiling   amongst the haze on the horizon

there is a quivering orange fruit   a blaze sinking into night
like an ark of some covenant   being carried away

fast feather-flash   a lammergeyer swoops past me   close
enough for me to hear air pass prayers through golden breast feathers

I can see the polished coffee bean of an eye   the dark taste of her gaze
outstretched wings nailed to swift air   talons grip a big thigh-bone
some feathery letter-shape circles   up away from me   my neck hurts

now as I crane upwards   she lets the big bone go

a white letter I (or figure 1) plummets   then explodes
bone-sparks on rocks   the lammergeyer falls following towards

food   now she is picking through the fragments
for marrowbone   I grit

my teeth

፮

beware the walia ibex   yea   behold this image   the orange coated beast
the black & white striped stockings   the swept back horns proud

as an ancient ship's bows   I say unto thee   surely it is within this goat-ship

within this ark of bones & muscles that the transparent stones of a god could reside
behold   the ibex with a tongue of green   a tongue of lobelia leaf that slowly

recedes into its mouth as it eats

I move closer to the escarpment's edge   one boot-toe hangs
over open air   to my left the cliff edge juts out as a promontory

suddenly on that promontory there is movement   a creature appears
on a small ledge thrust out into air   above brown valleys

balanced on an edge

a magnificent male walia ibex has taken a stance   his stiff black beard
below his chin like a paint brush   pointing downwards   and his stiff

tail like a black paint brush   pointing upwards   he is huge
nearly as tall as I am   his ribbed horns possess agile weight   they cut

open the air as he turns

his head to   gaze at me   now he plummets   drops
a full three metres to another tiny ledge   he is cantering along

a ramp that I would take many minutes to traverse   I hear
his hooves clatter like leather bells   he rushes as if the

sight of him is a secret

suddenly he is being

followed by a whole herd of his   kind   it's as if an orangey
brown river of ibex were falling   down the cliff   they gush

from the edge of the

promontory   many of them are whistling warnings at each
other because of my presence   far below me   the ship

-like male ibex leading the way

some of these muscular goats glance back up at me   the whole
herd gracefully falls   away into the depths below   the

escarpment's great

wave   their size dim   inishes

they are a faint orange   school of fishes darting   away
in   to the   shadows of the l   and's dry o   cean

፪

I crouch   my hands touch
the grass & the soil's dusty African fabric

a large troop of Gelada Baboons   just ahead
unbothered by me   many of them sitting
some lift their heads to glance
at my clothed form   but all stay
busy at their work   picking
through the ground   they crouch

to loosen roots with their teeth   and with long fingers
tug and tease the roots out   their hand movements
as delicate as if sewing   it's as if to feed
themselves they are picking apart

and skilfully altering the land's tapestry

I watch a nation of small furry people slowly moving
over their land   they are not human   but they *are*

people   a people perpetually & skilfully feeding themselves

and will do so as long their grass remains   as long
as rising degrees don't bring desert   close

to me now   a large male   he is facing me
the fine filaments of his fur & mane illuminated
backlit by sunshine   he is like a golden idol

but he is animated   he is not a statue   his face

is a black mask   he opens his mouth so
the whiteness of his teeth seems to make a bright sound
he observes me   he raises his eyebrows and his small

eyes see my eyes   he sees me see him   we both know

each of us knows our eyes have been seen   into
by the   other   only people know each other like this

on his chest a vivid red hour-glass of naked skin
it's as if his heart is bleeding   the red skin sings
its colour to the troop's females   it is an old song

            about new lives

but there are not many of these Gelada Baboons left
found only here in ancient Abyssinia's Simien Mountains
will it be more than a century before this tiny nation is gone?

Gelada Baboons with their wild voices that produce
such varied & complex patterns of sounds

will these beings evolve descendants   will they get our chance
to feel the   plea   sing   weight of whole words
in their mou   ths?

            and now a

tiny dark-furred baby baboon a   sleep yet clinging
to mother's back   the babe's thin tale
wraps like a vine   entwines with the thick

            ness of the mother's

February 2005

Lake, Needles, Thread & Paper

for Ariane

my legs move
like a waterfall
frozen

a lake tr   embles

as air flows
unseen

forms over water's skin

in darkness water's
vibration has a

bright sound

for company
on this cold walk
round death's rim
my bones of ang
er &

the acupun   cture
of winter birch trees
shallow-rooted

yet deep to lava

and full
of sky

each birch
has bright
paper bark

each birch feels
a world's soil

each birch
I pass
pricks white
pain truth
full as light's
speed

my legs grind
each step
like leav
ing & arriv
ing home like

ice boiling

I walk with fear
in my thighs
round a tre   mbli   ng lake
a world's ground
solid for miles
below me

sky's darkness miles high

yet there are
the birches &
the smoke of
wood burning wet

& there are star
-sharp need
les & a thread

of lightening for me

to ba   lance a
long across

the sound of
water towards
a friend's voice

& words:

take away
the paper

from your mouth

Andalucían Freight

Abejorro negro – dark jewel-blue
giant bee wobbling
on beautifully implausible wings
that blur blue like night sky, and buzz out
a deep drone felt cool

& vibrating against skin
like miniature breath or the passing
of one place into another place.

a kilometre or so across
the valley a rugged streak
of limestone-white
on the hillside
is suddenly washed
by cloud-filtered light
in a glowing blue moment
the shadow passes
and again white spills glare

Abejorro negro – splits
the daylight into every blackness.
Negredo near & beyond in one
sheen.

Black bee fascinated by pine spars
or chopped holm oak, or the eaves
of a human abode.
Bouncily hovering, monitoring textures
& scents for language-less messages &

tiny abysses
in which to deposit.

Abejorro negro – some say stings!

the ragged dazzling edge
of the rocky hilltop
opposite argues
with its solidity against
blue emptiness

Abejorro negro – gleaming
black-blue fragment of fantasy
carrying the burden of nothing
amongst olive-dapple &

Spanish lances of sunlight.

Forced Moment at El Torcal, Andalucía

The god and the beast
playing on the stone
together, the white stone,

Our reading-stone with its channels [...]
Peter Redgrove

And in short, I was afraid.
T.S. Eliot

This is a high plateau where deep time fights stone.
El Torcal is *karst landscape* – lime
stone performed upon by water & wind. A
medium
of sea-bed micro-bones & ground shells. Sculpted or
tortured?

Castles, towers, grey battleships, eroded sky
-scrapers, cracked sphinxes, fragments of moon, fossilised
galleons, ectoplasm petrified, solid ghosts of some
world's aeons, toppling temples, turds of gods, crowds
of still silence chatting & dancing, corridors

& crevasses for brambles & hawthorns.

A cabra montés on his limestone pedestal silhouetted,
the curved V of his swept
-back horns weapon-elegant. And across

the valley from him, beyond bleached chess-pieces
& wrecked battalions of stone, female mountain goats
atop blocks & spires, like look-outs, like
Classical statues but
alive & energised by pre-history's wild.

I scramble in amongst the grey maze
of buttresses & slots full of thorns & dark drops.
I get myself lost. Jump an irreversible gap.

Irresistible. Sweat erodes my face, shines
on my mask. I climb. I'm gleefully frightened –
night is not far off, and without light
the molars & fangs I clamber round will be closed
in a dark mouth. And I will have to curl
up cold amongst a god's teeth. In my fortieth
year – stay with stone; my delicate lime frame,
I hang my meat on, dried amongst compressed
& eroded remains of ancient tiny beasts. I struggle.

A small animated statue of my self in amongst
my own brain's maze. Folds, flaps & channels of stone.
Each jump or grip I make is me, me
as a thought of myself, a will across synapse.
I love this alive deadly dance through
some world's limestone cortex high on a plateau.

And I'm not alone.

I hear the leathery clatter of cabras' hooves.
I feel how bramble has scratched the back of my hand.
I see griffon vultures – two broad-winged soaring seekers, one
above me, the other a mottled blur in flow below.
I hear the clong-clonging of a sheep-flock's bells.

I smell my meat's work seep from my skin.
And from a crack in grey matter – a bright

azure & yellow-tongued iris rising
on a long stem of pale green light.

And I see my gentle friend standing, just beyond
the labyrinth's edge,
by a cream-dressed hawthorn, patient, waiting
until I ask for clues for release. I ask. She calls.

Her voice tells to me The Myth
of Exits. She gives
directions from a rim's perspective. And so

I climb down the last hard blob of brain – free
to step amongst brief flowers & crisp thistles.

Eye, Andalucía

Mapless, we head
for a mountain
not knowing its name.

But we have watched
the light change
on its flanks for days.

•

On the dark-soiled plain
the farmer gleefully foists
upon us fist-fulls
of his broad beans.

And with fast Spanish
and improvised sign-language
he asks
if we are to climb
the mountain on the plain's rim.

Si!
He hears we speak
no Spanish.

Agua, he exclaims,
and mimes
glugging
from a bottle,
he swings
his arm to define
a circle
on the ground,

he points
to the lime-white
mountain.

We think he means
there's a pool.

I shake his brown hand
and the calluses there
are like
a mountain range of years.

•

We have followed
the fire-break from
the plain's floor through pines
to the ridge.

We have fumbled & balanced
along the jostling blocks
of the limestone-paved crest,
the warm wind skidding
across our sweat-shined faces,
as minutes fattened hours.

We have gazed
at Malaga spread below along
the rim of The Med.

A ewe's head pokes up
from behind a white block.
Surprised, as us, she stares
with her dark slots. Clong

-clonging bells follow.

And a flock
with motley fleeces (splodged
browns, blacks & whites) rumbles
softly past us,
hooves tapping stone.

The shepherd has
the sun's words
brown on his face.

Folded over one arm –
a thick green coat;
folded over the other –
a strand of cloud
shaped as a frail

alive lamb.

He holds out this sheep-wisp,
and in fast Spanish, and
with his hands he asks
if we have seen
another scrap of lamb
along the ridge.

No! we shrug condolence.

His smile is like stone
with soft sun
passing over it.

He puts down el cordero –
it totters as if
the limestone is slick
with ice.

Agua, he exclaims,
and copies
exactly the performance
of the bean farmer below
who wrote
in neither Spanish
nor English, nor made
a mark on the ground,

but left a pool
in our minds.

•

Up here! cupped
by the bones
of a mountain – suddenly
a meadow
of fat grasses
& bright daisies,

and a pale beige disk
of shallow agua,
hazy as a cataract,
full of black
wriggling tadpoles.

And beside the blind pool –
a small but deep clear
well lined
with limestone cobbles.

A small frog *plohps*
into the mountain's

cold eye.

Lit Lichen, Tŷ Uchaf

we walk the track to Tŷ Uchaf

our Petzls solve
the dark around us so
we are surrounded by
a close cool bubble
of blue light

we are clothed
in a technological veil

we move
our bubble along so
keyhole sized portions
of a landscape repeatedly
develop and then
fade

away behind us and just

before Tŷ Uchaf
black & haw
-thorn forms spook
from inkiness into solidity
their plant-silence greets us

diode-lit lichen clings
tangled like fibrous silvery-green snow
to the convolutions
of their spikes & branches

it is a faint Christmas-ness
grown thick & Pagan

and balanced in the lichen's
green rinds glistening droplets watch
like numerous mouse eyes

we turn
the key in Tŷ Uchaf's lock
and we feel

in our minds behind
us (in the dark) the points
of thorns clogged
(or clothed?)
by frothy strands & splodges

of lichenous thoughts

Blackbird Stir

for Chris & Jo

in my friends' new house
in their attic between

two big brown bookshelves
randomly packed with poetry

I pass

sleep's pages through
my head and my head's

pillow is
a waking word

and the ajar skylight conveys air
as a bird's opening

of song

•

at one morning now
in a corner of beak

my entire life liquid
on a blackbird's tongue

long song-notes hold
a gloss house of sound

in the top of this voice-house
& light rhyming I sleep

I sleep between clear eaves
of soft death graceful

as one immortality's moment

•

outside in part-light's dim glee

outside over Sheffield's hills
houses' roofs flutter & flow

roofs like wings & beaks
with sleeping beneath

•

between two bookshelves
between two halves of beak
between attic roofs

I am in

a blackbird's dream

Bosigran & Rain, West Penwith

Bosigran crag is a face
of Under-Cornwall:

a granite smile meeting light;
a ground-mouth tasting sea.

Bosigran is a vast fossil
of some impossible lost beast.

Bosigran is where the land's frame is revealed.

Bosigran crag is a village
of blocks, cracks, roofs & slabs;

or a capsizing cathedral.

The villagers & priests & congregations, with their
metal ingots ringing & lurid ropes slithering, touch

the tilted streets of stone

with their fingers. They read
a sturdy & pure Book of biting Braille.

Bosigran is the rim of a crashed moon.

Bosigran crag is crinkled silver foil pulling
the whole Sun into the ground.

Hot Cornish light is tightened
here like a spring. But

today, just beyond
the white chess-piece of Pendeen Watch,

the sky is being lewd with the sea through
a swirling skirt of grey

railings all jangling. A squall
is coming our way. Within a blink

of the sky's eye
a shroud shivers across the crag. Instantly

Bosigran is a spilled jewellery-box;
a disarray of gems tumbling down its shelves.

All the rock-Braille shines, and where we touch
it it yields

to our fingers a slick subtext of snake-skin.

We are suddenly adventure-drenched,
your face hot with glee. We pick

our way across a sizzling moon.

Our clothes have become soaked ghosts
of our selves clinging

to our flesh. We cling

on to Bosigran's
glossy bone.

A Mapcraft

On a coastpath above
a frilly-white-lipped Atlantic,
just as that path clips
a broad zawn called a Western Blackapit,
on a west edge of a Forrabury Common
at around grid reference

SX093911,
approaching

a coastguard lookout over
a Boscastle Harbour, I notice,

around thirty centimetres from
that path's verge,
crossing a slatey stone,

a snail.

A single gazing
light-green vortex of shell,
fresh as new shoots, carried
by an almost-translucent
cream-yellow frilly-lipped foot
with see-through
glass-blown horns
oscillating slowly like sea
-weed in waves.

Bearing in mind we
are on our way
to a re-built village below

& its house
of cabinets & witches.

I think of
magic & act(.)

with my map,
in its clear
smooth plastic, I have
a power
to derange dimensions.

So,

gently I grip
a green-swirl-shell and lift
a vulva-soft snail up
out of its intricate landscape
and place

it onto a flat map.

And suddenly a snail
is a kilometre long
and slowly following
a blue thread of a River Valency,
heading for a papery sea:

slippery sexy edges
of its shifting shape slide,
on a salival membrane,

over a house
of witches & cabinets.

O slowly a flood of flesh passes;
and a map beneath plastic
for a moment suggests,
despite its precision & measurements,

a soft open myst ery.

Dead and Unburied at A Forrabury, A North Cornwall

At a church perched
above a Boscastle I sit

on a cracked
grave slab.

The crack runs across
the grave-resident's chest:
it runs straight

through a line of chiselled script;
and part-way along the line
one cunt-lipped ivy-leaf stands

out proud from the crack's dark.

A Kernow's flag crackles
on the breeze scraping round
a Forrabury Church,
and the weathervane fish swims
its metal silhouette stuck still.

The four black nights
& one crossed-day
of Kernow's cloth twitches
as countless molecules form
vortices across its texture.

I look seaward across
the top of a lop
-sided gravestone sinking in
to the hairy grass;

and beyond that grave's tilt
other stones arranged
as cracks of solidity
interrupting space.

A Celtic cross & its four
holes, each to be kissed
by tongues of wind;

and perched on top:
a frayed black poppet
of a crow (as if placed
by some film director's
penchant for cliché).

And as vast back
-drop a darkening sea-sky
with silvery chiselled
cloud-edges, and gulls
flashing their cross-bodies:

first of black against light
then of white against dark

as they swoop through
regions of ivory
-greys & slate-purples.

Now I stand

by a granite stone: shaggy
with chalk-green lichen. I stroke
my hand through the rough
growth, and feel

the cool wet of raindrops
the lichen has collected.

I watch drops roll,

and I remember

the straight black crack
on the grave-slab I sat
on some moment's aeon ago.

        if the slab
        were (or is)
        vertical

        the lip
        of the crack
        could be clung

        to with fingers
        strong as
        a rock

        climber's at
        least for a
        short while as

        the ivy

        lives rooted
        in the black
        of the gap

In amongst the tiny
lichen-tracery & erosion-swirls
on the slab's surface
I now notice

red mites, bright
as planets the size
of one fourth of a
salt-grain, wriggle
with what look like

random trajectories.

One mite,
perhaps-accidentally, follows
one chiselled channel
of a letter why.

    This could be or could
    've been or will
    be read

    as scrying; and the Y

    can or could
    be taken
    as a stang.

    I read
    and take

nothing,

as a Kernow's flag trembles
like a tongue
in some

eternity's mouth.

Serpent & Sea-Window, A North Cornwall

I

Just about to step
into a Tintagel Church's graveyard:

I'm first met

by a long-stemmed stone-bloom
of war memorial Celtic cross,
its cross-arms flared
fat as poppy petals.

Secondly I'm met

by a white lifebelt fastened
to a wooden cross. It's

as if graves are figures bobbing
on a surface of an otherside sea,
and this ring

is waiting to be thrown.
And the painted name
of the lifebelt's ship

is IOTA is

a tiniest amount of
hope.

And thirdly I'm met

by a flow of curves; by
a sea-wave writhe-glide
of snake crossing
the graveyard's entrance.

So much I want to touch!

I see his or her clear-inked
skin-shapes & adder-colours but
announce the presence of

a gra ssss nake.

So much I want to touch (It's just
a grasssnake!). I grip

his or her tail as she or he slips
into a crack between slates
in the graveyard's wall. I pull
very very gently ...

... cool dry smooth lightly-tiled skin
& muscle-tight vibration ...

... and suddenly slotted jewel-eyes &
a tiny yellow flick
ering of stang-tongue & dark
zag-zig-striped spine & his

or her head's

adder-pattern-warning.
And I real

ise I'm holding a viper.

I'm thrilled as a child riding a bird.

And I know I knew all
along what she
or he was I

so much
wanted to touch

II

There's a tight
ratchety zedding as
a young man stalks
a Tintagel graveyard's grass.

He's dressed in a day
glow yellow vest & orange
black-visored hardhat.

BUZZZZ knots
warm sea-air; forms
twines of sound writhing.

He's St George
strimming in the graveyard. I'm afraid

for serpents

III

inside the huge hollow stone cross
of a St Materiana

a Norman font
with heads crudely carved
at its four corners
all joined
by stone serpents
tails & heads up
curved (apparently

representing expelled
grace)

the thick smell
of creamy lilies

the chancel's
chessboard floor formed
from edges
of slate leaves cross
-hatched-&-packed tight

and glass-trapped
in stained-light
blond St George standing
horseless, holding

upright his
phallic lance

and his blood-crossed flag

IV

On a Glebe Cliff, towards
a Tintagel Head, I imagine

I'm bitten by a viper:

            starsh
            arp sun
            hot st
            ing in
            my fin
            gertip
            goes

supernova through my arm
my flesh inflates with
a writhing presence
my gut chucks out all
the parts of world I've
tried to pass through
me I'm stretched like
a pollen-cloud on wind
my brain sways like
a bloom of perfume
and my eyes bloodshot

roll as I roll
down slopes towards

a church of sea-cliff
& vast

dissolved-salt font

V

On the way from a Tintagel
to a Boscastle, on a cliff-walk

(suggested

to me by a poet called
Peter), opposite

a tall slaty Matterhorn
of sea-stack (named
on my map as Long Island)
streaked with gull-shit & meshed
round with flapping scraps
of gulls & their cries
like a pane
of moist glass squeaked
by thousands of fingers ...

I see

a sea-window in a steep
slate-stepped headland ridge;

a hole in ground sea
can be seen through an eye
to be threaded so

I climb down that ridge's
fragile rocks and pass

my whole body through

From a St Juliot to Beyond a Beeny, a Walk in a North Cornwall

by A. Mark Goodwin

if you are reading
this walk imaginatively
rather than actually
walking it then there is
only one certainty

this is a poem

an author of this
recommends for useful
& aesthetic accompaniment

OS Explorer Map 111
Bude, Boscastle & Tintagel
1:25 000 scale
Edition – B1
Revised for significant change 2003
Revised for selected change 2005
pertinent six-figure & eight-figure grid-references
& cardinal headings are given throughout

an author of this 'thinks' in both miles & kilometres
however, the overall (under-non) structure of the verse is kilometrical
(each kilometrical foot does not account for gradient, nor four-dimensional
space-time)

note that some one thousand seven hundred metres of walking
at a walk's beginning, and some five hundred metres of walking
at a walk's end have also not been accounted for

Itinerary

Kilometre One

St Juliot graveyard & church
hedge-tunnel on slopes above River Valency
a tractor, noticed across the Valency valley
leaving open pasture

Kilometre Two

meeting a couple in search of St Juliot Church
on the banks of the Valency, Minster Wood
sighting of dippers

Kilometre Three

young trout
lunch
where Valency valley widens to a flat bottom
blackbird heard, whilst leaving Minster Wood

Kilometre Four

dead shrew & sycamore key
stepping onto Boscastle's flood soak-away
entering Boscastle
The Cornish Rambler
cream tea at Harbour Light Tea Garden
The Museum of Witchcraft
a seeker & his mother
along the side of Boscastle Harbour

Kilometre Five

on Penally Point
looking at the Meachard, rocks off-shore
encounter with a sea slater
along slate shelves to zawn below Penally Hill
alcove carved in slate, & short rockclimb
a mother & her young son abroad
Penally Hill summit, & landmark for shipping

Kilometre Six

over grass slopes towards Pentargon Bay
a grieving woman
resting above Pentargon Bay
examining a Beeny Cliff
grasses moving, near & far
seven seals in Pentargon Bay
a plum, and sharing water
descending steps towards Pentargon Falls

Kilometre Seven

crossing Beeny Stream, & Pentargon Falls
ascending steps away from Pentargon Falls,
& a hidden slate-alcove
assumptions above a Beeny Cliff
strange convex slopes

Kilometre Eight

approaching Fire Beacon Point
ascending Fire Beacon Point
summit of Fire Beacon Point, & two men & a boy
view of Buckator Cliff & Gull Rock
inland to Higher Beeny, & hollow-way
gorzy slopes above Beeny Stream

Kilometre Nine

honeysuckle scent
prehistoric plants, and stepping over Beeny Stream
wading through dry grasses
encounter with brown horses

SW128912
heading east

... tree-foliage coils
like green froth
across a St Juliot

tree-like across

Church, stone
feelers of finials poke
up from breeze-
vibrated leaf-spray

stone poke
breeze-spray
waits me

a giant snail waits
for a her & a me

to our left or north

a slope of coppery-
green-barley-sheen each
wind-touched
ear conveys
waves of sense
tive tremblings a
watery flow of
crop in chaos pran
sing & trickling like lit
flood lapping at
our thighs as
we walk a
hedge path

green-wind-ear

lit at
as a
path

at slope-top a hedge-crest
where wind-bent hawthorns curl
like surf

curl surf us

above us

so my friend I love & a me are below
slant-lit green

at a bottom of a field

we are under
neath

summer's growth for us floods a
Lea-on-Ness

whilst a St Juliot's snail feels sky

we neath
summer's
lea whilst
set rime

set hundred
rime starlight set hundred

bechance I prophet
wisest bechance

I came magic marked
rare back magic

°

we enter a churchyard by crossing
a cool dark slate stile

and we are met by granite
a face of a Celtic cross
for a moment with a mouth-hollow
as shadow announces a trick
this cross has a drowning gasp

granite cross-hollow trick gasp

and I don't notice
a light-grey grave
of my namesakes

it is my friend I love who points
out buried Goodwins an I knows nothing of
Lesley John & Brenda

are dead strangers

strangers' taps

a she taps
gently their grave-granite with
her rough-cut hazel
walking stick
but it is me

that spots bolted
to the headstone's edge
a snail-shell moment
arily shaped

me bolted edge
moment shaped

like a coil in which
to worship

in a St Juliot graveyard

o

inside a slippery silence
of a St Juliot an I reads outloud
by engraved glass light's
watery poetry
tugging & deep as gone

silence outloud lights
poetry gone

my voice & another's words
together are dead & alive

whilst the woman I love captures
digitalised photons in her camera
making replicas of a faint
solidity we exist with & in
a she photographs a clear
pony-&-rider-shaped
space of glass

faint in clear

in a St Juliot church

cleverly she overlays
a ‘real’ green beyond
glass bearing
silvery negatives
of an engraver’s vision
a miniature
St Juliot with Kernow’s
flag inverted
(black-cross on white
cloth) floats over
a world outside a church
beyond salivas of worship

overlays beyond
bearing negatives

white over church

I push a whole
length of my arm through
my watery eye
into a little abyss in my skull
I feel
about for an invisible
gleam cupping
my life but it remains
hidden as my wrist aches
with cold

whole through eye

plunge water sharp
from hence real
know leaves little spans
solid scoop runlet
kingdoms boiling since
gives real plunging
water under where
darkly now drinking down
lover walked
blue burn placed
rim drunk copse rinse

sharp real spans

sank plumbed glass arm
bowl awakens
used pool face face intact sung
pattern plants day intact
presence sung
touched
sipped

she pays a pound
for a faint yellow pamphlet
all about a St Juliot Church

she for all
and for
a window

and she pays a pound
for a pamphlet about
a Thom Ash-Ardy Memorial

Window

and in a visitors' book an I writes
an entry in a July of a 2009
with what I hope is love
and not a poet's arrogance:

churches are so
snail-like
hard stone shells so like shells
& soft gentle silence silence bells
& slippery bells

today on the slope to The West
of Saint Juliot's

snail

a crowd of barley stands
all heads bowed & stroked
in one direction by

the wind

snail stands stroked
by wind sin feels
ground

for barley does not sin
just feels

the ground

°

now the woman I love, & an I, begin to follow
a Valley of River-Through-Mill down
towards a Vast At L'Antic

now a towards we

we walk away from a great stone snail

and she invites
me to follow close
to a hedge-edge
of a pasture where
cattle have poached
ground grassless
and various branches
hazel hawthorn oak
bow low like a tunnel
she walks crouched
in a green surf-curl
stepping over dried
fat pats

she in stepping

I prefer grass
& a raised path

grass path passage

SW126912
heading back west

I watch her passage

each of her steps
respects beasts
she is so
beautifully creaturely
following
where creatures have been
light sifted
by twigs & leaves
flakes across

i & i
each
respects
she

sifted leaves across moment

her living this moment

now a sharp
slice of loss

cold glass syllables from a poem's ghost

a thin
length of
abyss
for a split
second slips
through
my chest

thin of abyss-split lips

passes
I blink

she's still
here with me

living our moments

°

we pass on
down a valley
westwards
with a Valency
in its vale veiled
by leaves below us

Valency veiled us
with in by

a River Valentia
of power competence
be well & strong
a combining power

of an atom
a number
of atoms
an atom

can
dis

place or
bond with

place bond

our boots on grass
across fields
and she has noticed
on steep slopes
across-valley from us
a little tractor
working stripes
of cut grass
its engine silent
like a dreamt toy
but a living man
miniaturised

stripes grass-silent

SW123913

to unseen
by distance

unseen distance
to by we must be

we know
must be driving must
be one making

hay
unless

driven
by a woman or a
girl or a boy

we pass on
from open fields
we from to
to footpath hemmed
in by bush & tree
and to our north
or our right
close contours darken
darken steepness reading
a paper with steepness
reader I'm reading

a map
and you're reading
a me reading that and

that's a perhaps

SW121913

under our feet now
1km are path-pebbles
& bits trees lose
bark-dust & leaf-fibres
& fragment-shades as

now pebbles lose fibres as slip

light-lines slip
through leaves
above her & a me and rinse
beams through air

a couple approaches us

his crisp blue shirt
(with buttons neat
as his intellect shining
from his gentle eyes)
brings sea-blue fresh
from a Bosc Astle below
especially as
green-light-slants
glance his cloth
his beard keeping
years trimmed
to his face
his smile young
in a middle of a life

from brings
from especially
green glance

and she
is years his senior
shades round
as seal-eyes hide
her eyes
her black trousers
& blouse blaze
against a yellow
scarf tied round
her throat's
soft oak-bark
and her feet
dainty in black

round throat's bark
feet black

ballet-esque slippers
she moves
with stern peace
says only silence

silence mother-certain

probably his mother
I'm certain

he loves her

and now he gives his voice
soft but clear & solid
English spoken from
a southern throat
& book-formed mind
and there's a kindness
in his tone & eyes

from throat
mind-kindness

they're in-search of
St Juliot Church &
their own versions
of a poet & his grief

of & versions

he asks us
a way

us way

I try
to explain
an I describes
entering
open fields
and aiming
for a hidden
slate stile

in a dyke
& a faint
trace of foot
-flattened grass
across a corner
of pasture
that leads
to hidden

faint foot grass

pasture leads hidden

but he has
no map
and I know
without it
a way
is easily missed

I
without
way

as I think
of showing
him a code
on paper

code paper passed

they have passed

already twenty metres
to east and we
twenty metres west

and on our way

o

a Valency widens
and our path now touches
its banks as
a Minster Wood full
of tall bible-barked

way widens touches
as full barked holds
pale fractured by shadows

but sappy parishioners holds
swathes of leaf-pale
underlight fractured
and dotted by
brown shadows

we step down
from a bank path
onto slate shelves
river water has
bevelled

shadows down path

late selves

slate's dry grey
& wet blue-dark
& silvered water-lit edges

& seen noise, solidified
to clear liquidity obeying
gravity's imperative
& water's will
of circles, flows
like nothing spoken
for a first time forever
an undulating sheen
of crystalline yet
gelatinous light
slides-&-rolls tight

edges solidified obeying
imperative will
flows spoken forever

chaos over
layered pages
of still slate

light tight over pages

& each little slate
-lipped abyss
seen or unseen

in this river slips
its location slips
its placeness slips

slips slips slips 'imagine'

through 'imagine'

shall an I lie
down
in a shallow
and let
a whole glide
of river
sluice through
my skull's
orbits
shall an I see
shall I

I see I
river eyes

see with river
my eyes
stretched
everglides
of water-miles
soft ribbons
of molecules
rubbing gently
along
my sockets'
bone rims
shall I see all
lit shallows
& black
abysses pass
as my skull's
cleaned

shallows black pass skull
's cleaned see-glint

shall an I see
a glint
cupping
shall I see
a lost
nestling gleam
at bottom
of mind
how will
I breathe I
pull

shall a nestling at of how

from water
shallow but
utter other
no further
no more
an I can only

from shallow
utter no
no I

see a solid
world through solid
eyes I see
through moist
mollusc-soft
organs of solid
flesh

solid solid see

a brown-backed
white-bibbed yet
kingfishery smudge
of bird wing-whir darts
down-stream low close
to slate & water what
was that shot across
eye-corner?

smudge darts

we follow
ecstatic as cats but
not with hunter's hunger
this sudden fast scrap
of flesh lit by life

attracts our lives

lives perched

now there are two perched
on a low branch close
to water-flow
both dip close flow dip

up dip
down dip
up down dip
dip down up
dip ...

and the glee

the glee of the woman I love
her creature-inspired glee
clear as alive
flows

glee love glee
alive flows
now flows

flows now
now flows

2km

we pass on

°

further down
water widens
further where

SW112909

dark green
shuttle-shadows of
young trout hang
in flow mouths
open to up-
stream they'll grow
on what river
flow brings

mouths up-grow river

suddenly hungry
we sit to eat
from our plastic lunchbox
strips of cut cucumber
tomatoes & houmous
& sweet energy bar
our stomachs' hollow
mechanisms trans
form molecular patterns
to fuel our walking

hollow trans-patterns walking

°

we walk on

walking on
paper part

on paper
contours part
as a valley-bottom
begins to broaden
our boots chlink
on slate-scree
coppice-clumps
of young hazels
sprout from this
metallic-chipped
& glinting ground
thistle gorse heather

SW104911
flat valley bottom

purples & yolk-yellows
sun-inflated fragrance
presses our skins
and we talk of water
released from sky
to moor then shed
to be constrained
by ground's narrow
grooves accelerated thrust
to a boiling
brown liquid plough
vicious & fast passing
to rip at trees here
& people's houses down
river

yellow's fragrance skins water

sky shed constrained

passing here down

a blackbird's
wet notes now
deepen space

°

and we pass on
towards a mass
of metallic glints
& jangling colours
we can see
a Bosc Astle's
car-park where
a Minster Woods
ends to relinquish
a world of leaf
-crisp wild & leaf
-blurred histories
& myths

blackbird's now space
on mass glints colours

where woods relinquish leaf

now

3km

she photographs
a flat dead shrew
& pale green
sycamore key
framed together
on bare earth-dust
feet have scuffed

shrew green key
together dust-scuffed

o

at a car-park
some other

other starts step

side starts
we step

SW100912
Boscastle's car park
& flood soak-away

from dirt onto
plastic

water-porous matting
Bosc Astle's new

car-expanse
now our boots

expanse boots senses

slap Tarmac our senses

are flooded an abundance cars buses children's ice-cream instincts elderly glad & chatty in pastel blouses or sullen in brown cardigans & trousers pierced teenage girls & their aching boyfriends men with office-hard faces starting to soften women away with home's weight following them feet in sandals & heels & town shoes & boots fit for hill & coast & wide windows full

of hope but
contorted to Cornish kitsch some

place awash
with currency's hurry
a flow-through
of flesh & minds

contorted place
with a 'of'
lives a 'through'

lives
a surge

through pasts'
museum-cleaned &
theme-park-fresh traces

brand-new quaint
cobbled modern-old-world
CGI-sharp bowed
stone walls &
crooked roofs a

quaint world bowed

kit
of old
parts
just

parts just

finished
glue newly
cured

a set
for an in
ex
orable flow
of us extras

SW098912
in Boscastle

ones of one-place-now
elide
ones of one-place-was
Bosk Astle
Bo Scattle astle scattle stalls cattle
Bosca Stalls
Bog Cattle
a flow

of ho
ly days
gone fl
ows be
low hol
ograma
tic ho
pes

count
less tran
sparencies
of Boscastles
slip-flow over
each other through over through held here
all these minds held
in this flood of flesh here
a flood
of versions
versions' floods
including

floods in
cluding me
I it

for me
because I
red it
& in a few

seconds
for you now
because
you will
hear/
read this:

a Peter Red

grove's plump   red plump doors
volume of doors
& windows
called a Bos
castle Sea
Visit & a Dune
from a Virgil
Caverns

mew air new room
bedroom of Dune *there*
pages includes Boscastle   mew bedroom pages
shut on it open
whole room year
any season unpredictably
gull-call itself
eyes sill beak grey waves
feathers breath sea mew
everything pages   any gull eyes
feathers everything

room there Boscastle open
year unpredictably itself
waves mew pages

open itself pages

pages pages pages

pages

°

we nip in
to an out
door gear

we to door

shop called
A Cornish
Rambler

on hangers
are high
-tech fibres

arranged
as possible
ghost-shapes

in which
to clothe out
door selves

which out selves

shirts trousers
jackets boots
hats socks

The Cornish Rambler
The Bridge
Boscastle
Cornwall
PL35 0HE

patient as
dead wait
to be bought

and brought
alive by
walkers

along a
Cornish
edge of

by walkers a Cornish of world

a world

°

and we pass on

towards scones
& a Harbour Light
Tea Garden

light garden liquidly

sun deepens liquidly
dazzling on white plaster
we sit in a dry harbour
of gated patio
with low slate walls
in front of a re-build
as a Valency flows
to sea through
a rebuilt riverbed

build flows through
riverbed warmth

with warmth
on my arms I imagine
fast cold
brown water &
where we're sitting

under
and taken

under taken sea

away to sea

SW097913

Harbour Light Tea Garden
The Harbour
Boscastle
Cornwall
PL35 0HD

harbour light dim
below liquid tonnage
a dark garden of currents
& ugly blooms
of turbulence
& terrified people's
prayers

"But what of the little shop?
Trixie new that God wanted
her to rebuild ...

... almost identical
to the original, complete
with dipped
roof & intentional

slipped slate.

The Harbour Light Tea Garden
was opened in October
a year of our Lord 2006.

We thank our Lord
Jesus for all
His blessings &
favour & for
this Harbour Light
He has given us
to show
His love & grace."

opposite us
& our pot
of tea & delicious
softly cratered
& creamed moons
doors
of a Museum
of Witchcraft
pull in in
quisitive people
(a flood-height
line is clearly
marked along walls
amongst
cabinets & saved
pagan past
-ness)

moon's doors

The Museum of Witchcraft
The Harbour
Boscastle
Cornwall
PL35 0HD

and suddenly
our blue-shirted
St-Juliot-Church-searcher
is lamenting his lost way
back up where a Valency's
width was less than
a man's or woman's height
they didn't find
a slate stile or feel
its cool grey they
were drawn down
by inclined pastures
to riverbanks

suddenly shirted
searcher way

they will try
another day

try day worth say
poems & glass
recommend map

it's worth
the effort I say
there are poems
in the church &
engraved glass
I recommend
an OS map

and now
that we've
finished and paid
for our re
fresh
ment we pass
on on

fresh pass on wave

our way & wave

at a seeker's companion in black
with yellow at her throat
& sunglasses-seal-disks
who's drinking tea and
eating cake as part
of today's parts
of a world
she'll consume
to live
and who
I'm certain
is a searcher's
mother
he'll have to
seagulls scream
lose soon

black throat disks
& part parts

certain searcher's mother

er or later un
less she loses
him first

°　　first surf heard

surf
can just be heard
as we walk towards
a Pen Ally Point
a narrow harbour below
rippling gently as fresh
Valency meets salt
soft glugs & sloshes against
carved slate blocks
two stubby buffer-piers
like pin-ball flippers form
a kind of valve between
calm human harbour &
utterly careless sea

SW095914
Boscastle Harbour

below fresh salt
against blocks

soft carved two
like a calm utterly

and at the end

4km

of a Valency's S
-bend mouth
a block of slate

-silhouette-face balanced
sphinx-like on headland watches
a river shed its fresh
ever-selves into sea's
vast question

a silhouette-sphinx a
ever vast now

now we balance

as wind tampers
with our centres
of gravity

centres gravity slate

SW093915
Penally Point

over tilted slate
footworn-rounded along
a ridge of a harbour's
defending headland towards

that black gazing block

to our south or to left
grey-green sea undulating
like slaty jelly
whilst to our right or to north

jelly north marine cream writhing

lit-brilliant ultra-marine
& laser-white surf-cream
of inhaling/exhaling writhing
annihilating & alive Atlantic

and now salt
-spray lights
salt lights memory dad
a memory
of my dad
as young man
canoeing ferocious
dad man ferocious sea
Cornish sea
his strong
arms glistening he pulls
his wooden blades
digs hard
into angry green &
roaring
white his red canoe flung
and looped &
his faint
flung & faint
but powerful
spray-hiss-faded whoop
of joy

I chew a sprig of samphire
aromatic hot & salt grows   samphire grows ghost ocean
in my mouth like a ghost
or momentarily compressed ocean
then fades to tint
my saliva
                                  tint saliva slicks

salt-greased wind slicks
our cheeks and
rattles our clothes
                                            clothes shattering over

and to west seagulls shattering
their wet-glass voices over
a hogsback rock of a Mea Chard
or May Shard like a slate
ship capsized
or huge Unterseeboot
rising

then far
beyond this fragment of land an ocean-curve
of a planet's horizon
                                  far curve horizon friend
and my friend
I love has found
in a crack in slate
a plump woodlouse-like creature
segmented-&-grey as its slate realm
I pick
                                        realm pick world

up this miniature first world
war battle-tank inch-long arma
dillo-ey living cathedral with thick
jointed feeler-finials shim
mering with hyper
sensitive touch an I can just

feel its claws grip
my skin and I know
in this moment (really
know) I can never know
what it knows of my skin
& arm-hairs it now
trundles amongst

just grip know

skin now amongst knows(') once

(all an I can know is its name (it knows
nothing of) or at least know once
an I gets home and can
Google it

to find: '*Ligia oceanica*, the sea slater,
is the largest of the British woodlice, reaching
a length of up to 30 mm (1.2 in). It is found
on rocky shores throughout the British Isles.
Its wider range extends from Norway to
Morocco, and has since been introduced
to North America [across an ocean].' (My
note.))

reaching found isles

we return
slate's creature
to its maze of slots
& tilted surfaces
we turn

away from a block
of a slate sea-gaze
& answer-less riddle

°

return creature slots
surfaces turn
block gaze riddle close
along lichen streaked leached
to perched
walled zawn dark
lolls sea's milk

SW09489169
zawn below Penally Hill

follow a path close
to cliff-edge along
slate shelves lichen
-spattered & streaked
slipperily with leached
ground water to
a path-end perched
above a black-walled
white-watered zawn
where a shiny dark
seal-shape lolls
in a dazzle of sea's
simmering milk
and my friend

is so thrilled
to see a shape
of her self
on her sea's
creaturely mirror
she shouts
seal seal seal
I love her
so much as
she makes
her sea-wishes
to be
another being she
or a she of her
needs but
I know she
would never
willingly leave
me for her
sea she stays
to be

thrilled shape self sea's
mirror shouts

a person
with a
person
of me

be person a person me

I step down
uneven slate
shelves towards
sheer space above
chaos's swirling
wet patterns
& vortices of noise
one wrong

swirling patterns noise
wrong & gone

step and
I'd be gone

bright sunlight
on my skin
salty moist air
in my lungs
wind's slide
moving my hair

and no
time or distance
away from this
existence is

no distance this
is gone

gone

carefully my life's
clear gleam
& its body climb back
up from infinity's lip

whilst my friend
I love watches
& trusts

her courage

sat together now
clinging fast
now fast each we
to a ground & each
other we

stare at white
forced water press
fast against black slate
obliterating black
with dazzle and
sizzling away leaving
writhing lace black
sizzling writhing grows fades
grows through as white
fades and then
again inflates fast
blasts like
polar bears pouncing
and then smashed fast
to soft airborne fur
& fluttering feathers
& white scurrying mice as
slate like night gleams
slate sea again
sea-polished and then
again white fast &
black fast & fast black &
fast white entangled &

cri
& & & cri cro su
ss-cro
ssed & su

ddenly I under
stand Ker
now's flag a f
lapping of en
twined dry & dren
ched gone &

now's lapping twined

here
fast &
fast ...

o

a map's orange
/brown contours here
are close-&-cluttered with
thorns that denote
escarpment
steep slopes abut
light paper-blue sea
on which is printed
Penally Hill
its y's tail grazing
symbols for flat rocks
run through
with Mean High Water's
thread of grid-line blue

grazing rocks through water's blue

and also in brown
/orange is a Penally Hill's
summit spot-height 88
metres above a sea's level

we climb steep tufted grass
sea's soak-thuds less
heard more felt as faint
earth-jolts

faint jolts found carved

SW095916

and now she has found
a niche-seat carved
in slate-cliff sun's
heat leaking from it
a lozenge of hollow
holding a single
-thousands of invisible
sea-watcher
an upright grave
for alive gazer
a cul-de-sac of solid
slate gated with
sea-sky's vast space

hollow single invisible watcher
grave gazer solid with space

I climb by drawn
by broken rocks
leave her seated
to scramble arrogantly
amongst a plump
upholstery of fragile
but stubborn coast plants
sea-pinks & stiff sea-grasses
flaky-slate-&-shaky-blocks
entrance a me I
concentrate entirely on staying
alive and live
in a lit instant of dance
& thinking

I staying live dance thinking me

she meets me
at outcrop-top

my hands not touching
ground as ground tilts
away from vertical
walking again

vertical again through easy

our boots scuff through
coarse grass until easy
foot-stunted path-grass towards
a Pen Ally Hill's summit plateau

°

and we pass

a mother & her young son
her long dark hair wind-wavering
his round olive face ablaze
with new place
his accent perhaps Spanish as
proudly he declares "I have been

to the tip of Britain!" and I
shout back "Wonderful!" the word
stretched away on wind my

son wavering ablaze
place as been
I word my
pattern dispersed

breath's pattern
of sound dispersed
amongst incomprehensibly vast
amounts of molecules

and I think of my own
son & his smile's blaze
& his nearly ten years of
newness to world (his
birthday's in early August) only
ten years since he did
not exist he has
bones & blood &
a live ghost so
much his

and son & newness

blood ghost

°

we pass
on now reach

a Pen Ally Hill's
summit landmark conspicuous
to distant shipping
a tall thick white pole flying
a flat metal fish stiff
in wind-current
a pole shivers three
fat steel hawsers kee
ping it in place an I
hangs from one my
hands plugged-in
to wind-vibration
sky sliding I cling
to rigging

conspicuous shipping
flying stiff current

SW096916
Penally Hill
spot-height 88m

less
than 800 m due
south from here give
or take a few
degrees across a deep
time-&-water-gouged   gap
of a Bosk Astle's valley a
Forr Abury's Church pokes
its white flagpole sky

deep gap a pokes sky

wards & flies
a Kernow Cross and I
know, although too small
to see from here, its
weathervane is

also a
fish high
in air
making

a high air making

sea
of a
sky

two little
air-fish guard
a Valency's
exit & entrance

a Pen Ally Hill's flagpole
-fish is perhaps a
cod or a haddock
it's long with a frill
of fins along its back
my brother would know
he's a chef and knows
his fish and knows
how to catch-&-gut-&-cook
such

flagpole a haddock frill

know knows knows
cook such now

I imagine him now

my brother on his other side
of a world at night in a
winter Australia while here
it's day he's asleep
as I'm awake
and soon

we'll swap I'll be
dreaming as he feels
his realness I miss
him

dreaming his him

°

SW099916
heading east north east

now we follow our
way over rounded
5km grass slopes towards
a cleft landscape of
a Pent Argon Bay where
sea's ages have eaten
deep into hill

sea's deep sitting

sitting on a stile
is a woman, her long
blond hair writhing in rushing air

from this distance
she is unclothed
bones & her dog's frame
naked of flesh gleams
in ages-old sunlight
she stares at sea
she is a skeleton grieving
her grief eat
ing lit air
she stares to sea
her bone dog jumping
up at her raw self
she stares sea
her loss bright white
strands writhing from
her skull

distance unclothed
frame gleams sunlight

sea grieving
eat air
sea jumping
self sea
white from skull

now closer to her
I see she is breathing
is fleshed & not
nude bone

her face is gently creased
her eyes lit with sea-light
she smiles a soft sturdy
peaceful sadness &
stung gladness perhaps

bone-creased light
sturdy & perhaps

she's a widow

widow stone rounded

her stone
loss rounded
soft by a wash
of millions of minutes
in a sea of years

she dismounts from her stile
and we cross past her
her cream Labrador drawn
instinctively towards
my creaturely friend I love who
pats and fusses pleased
for her hands to be licked

dismounts cross

pleased licked sheltered wind

now we rest sheltered
from wind
our backs pressed
against a drystone wall's
warm slate

we're on a lip of
a Pent Argon's cleft

slate of cleft-pent froth

SW10859189

300m wide with pent
sea silvered with froth
bright as fluorescing argon

and facing us is a cliff
beetling blue-black storm
-ravaged layers cradling   storm cradling rising verge
scree-slopes rising
300ft from froth to verge
a cliff given

no name

on my map but named
as a Beeny Cliff
in my North Devon &
Cornwall rockclimbing
guidebook with one
route recorded called
The Tourist, 530ft,
Extremely Severe 5b
+ A2 first climbed
in an October of a '79   five dubious phrases
five long pitches of
dubious slate including
phrases like 'climb
up via a loose wall to gain
the second scree slope'
even when fit &
rock-tuned this cliff
of dark sharp choss   choss-pushed ardour
would've pushed
my snailish ardour
for adventure back
into my life's shell

I am tired my
limbs ache from
not too many miles I'm
rising
though from a
body hollowed
through nearly two
viral-ill years' veils
of dis
solving selves this
pushing of muscle a
gainst ground & gra
vity is now giving
my soul's body
back to me

my from I'm
rising
a hollowed
two

and my friend I love

she nursed a me
to here to
here-ness her
body by mine on
an edge above other
ness I place

me to her on other place

my hand on her hip's
slightly fat-plushed
skin

and as she
eagerly energised
as a child eye-gleans
a Pent Argon's surf
for seal-kind my
hand rests

rests like a tired
bird or vole on
her woman's
body strong
with her soul

hand rests bird
her body with close-bobbed

close grass-heads wind
-bobbed knit
a peace-pattern through
my weariness & wave
ring grass across
bay at some

distance shows sheen

& shade
liquidly repeating
tumbles like unseen
people &
creatures she

wind knit through wave
across some sheen shade
repeating unseen & she
counting below sea's o
she through as each

is counting
her seals below
seven in sea's
swirls of o
ther world she
is shot through
with animal as
each

dark doggy
head or mer
maidish body

resolves in surf

doggy mer-body surf she shear

see she
sheen sheer

she shry
soaked shrines

eyes rise she
shines she sure

she sure taste

and a taste
of plum I'm
eating now
glows rouge
in my mouth

in my mouth
a fruit from
a living plant and

mouth from & world through

a part of world

to pass through
myself's flesh
flesh that's part
of same

and the woman I love
is solid by
a body of a man
of me

now we share
from our water-bottle
to pass
a stuff of sea &
river through us

a touch of un
touchable & in
visible gleam
in dark abyss

to a river
a touchable visible

I hold this
happiness
like all sky
& sea in
side one
second's shine

sky in one shine

as an

other poet's
grief or
version
ripples

sapphire high
loved below
engrossed
light cloaked
levels again
beauty go
said chasmal
elsewhere cares

high below
engrossed cloaked again
go chasmal cares

o

it's time
we were
on our
way so

we repack
our rucksacks
and begin

it's we on way
we our
and descending

descending
earth-packed
plank-bolstered
steps down steep
vale-side ten

SW108919
& environs
heading north

contour lines
a descent
of fifty
solid-world metres
in four flat
map-millimetres or
a drop of one

solid in map

hundred & sixty
-four feet in one
hundred & nine
horizontal yards

I aim my boots
at each wooden
step-edge my
6km precision fading
with each
weakening knee-bend
I check my by-now-
too-familiar dismay
two years ago I
was young

boots wooden my fading

enough to have run
up (never mind
walk down) this
valley-side ladder
but too young to be

young rung mind

this ladder be now

me now
I step

across a Bee Ny Stream
that follows a line of least
resistance in a V
-corner formed by valley walls

I across that resistance corner

directly to our left or to west
a Bee Ny stream is trans
formed by precipice
into a Pent Argon Falls
a drop of one hundred
& twenty feet on a calm

a formed into a

day after rain has fattened
flow a long white rope
with a frayed-spray end
would waver over
moss-glistened ledges
but today

flow with would

a fast cliff-draft pushes
fall-water upwards so
cliff-edge grass wriggles
wetly conveying drops
from verge to air a curl
like wave breaking forms
as stream leaves

cliff wetly from like
as ground returned

ground to be
returned as spray my
cheeks cool and there's
a gentle wet-patter
on my rucksack's fabric as
wet-sunlit-air
rushes

now we follow
a short detour path
to a viewing platform
a patch of foot-scoured
earth tucked in
to a Pent Argon Bay's
northern corner and
slung out on jutting ground

from here a fall's glistening
liquid phantoms clearly seen
jumping back up
over cliff-lip to spread
selves through grass as
watery gauze

glistening seen
up-spread as gauze

but my friend I love
will not turn
her face from
bright shimmering cream
turbulence cradling
dark torpedoes of seals'
bodies & buoys
of their heads

turn from cream cradling seals

I tell her to stay
for a while I'll
go slowly ahead
to begin to climb
steps upwards

I for go to steps

o

each step up
is a slow stretched thud
of ache through thigh muscle
faint footmarks off
to left draw a me off
-route round a ridge
I find a slate-alcove
I sit slate hard
on my buttocks an I watch
es a Bee Ny Stream and wish
es to flow soft-sure
as water I best
check she
doesn't miss me
I return to a ridge-crest
just above where an I left
our agreed route she
is working up steps
I shout & wave she's
seen a me so I go
back to wait for her
in my little cave

hard watch wish

crest left
she steps
she's go
her cave bee
pulls to

Bee
Ny Stream pulls
my eyes to

slow lengths valley
sides erode
fossils come

valley erode come

& go I
've gone

soft sleep-weight
pins a shape
of mine to a time
only pelvic-slate-pain
connects a me
& keeps

gone weight-shape
time-pain me keeps

I rub my eyelids scrunch
my forehead skin re
focus my eyes my
mind wakes up
again where

6:7:09 AD 1807hrs

is she? only

mind again is cold

cold slate
next to me
in this alcove
I'm watching
myself get up
now rush over
my detour-ridge
to coast path I
watch a self of
me search for her
below but her
seal-lookout is empty
she must've gone
on ahead mist
my turn off miss
understood my
wave-&-position

empty gone mist

in this little
bit of world
I'm cross with her
she should've
looked harder
at where I was
on a ridge in
relation to her
position I rush
along coastpath
to my left a
Bee Ny Cliff
edge juts words
beetling jut chasmal
jut chasmal beet
ling words flung
lost like ashes
chasmal jut beet
ling a silhouette
of thorn on edge
above abyss she's
really naughty for
not navigating
properly for not
knowing what my
wave meant I'm
furious with a

self of me for
assumptions and
dark sharp lengths of
smashed sky slip
fast down
through soft evelight

position little world

I'm she
looked at
on relation

her rush coastpath

to be edge

jut ling lost

edge she's for navigating

furious self

dark smashed fast through this

SW107920
possibly top of Hardy's Beeny Cliff
certainly top of climbers' Beeny Cliff
heading west

this is
an evening coastpath
on a Corn
ish clifftop not

on ish tracts

tracts of time -&- us gone

I'm alive now
and there she is
approaching me
her face scrunched
cross like mine
her face a puddle with
my wavering face
on her surface we
with face we she
re-run events she
has been ahead
perhaps now done
an extra K and done & descent
re-climbed a descent
I'm cross she's
pushed herself she's
as tired as I am why
didn't she notice
my position I'm

cross over
nothing over nothing know
know

assumption's traps
so shutup

we agree how easy
it is to miss
a way

how hidden
abysses have
trivial lids
how our steps cross
over nothing

we kiss and we
're on our
°

way a   we our a

path of slate-shards traverses
wide convex slopes
of monotone
beige-grassed heath

SW105922
heading north
then north east

we've entered
a suspended
expanse of rounded   suspended rounded cut
ground cut

off by coastal-curve
behind & before
us & above   curve before above fades below
slope-curve fades
to sky & below
I know unseen
cliffs plunge only felt
as slight thuds of
sea-crash
or at least

an I & we & you
can imagine
we feel that

we follow a filament balanced

imagine that balanced sky

between sky
& sea we are

specks like alpinists
specks on sea's horizontal
on a high altitude snowfield
sea's vast vertigo a
horizontal of vertical
our tiny figures

a vertical figures space
distance distances us

are condensed space
we are distance
we are distances
distance is us

we are only seen

by sky's
& sea's

we by & too blue

too wide
blue eyes

wide eyes paper

on paper
we are now
SW10709260
on a green
coastpath diamond
just by a B
of Beeny Cliff (printed
parallel to coast)
and just under
printed coast under ending
a blue e ending
Seals Hole

7km

on paper we're approaching
a Fire Beacon Point
flat rocks of
Beeny Sisters detached
to north are
represented like
cracked bone fragments

approaching point of detached

western hair
loved waves
ceaseless clear
flew dull purples
Beeny again say
wild ambling laugh

waves' clear purples say laugh

opal woman
woman mews
sky laughed cloud
Atlantic sun
all shall
sweet still woman
knows

sea free me
away
say day
rain stain main sky
nigh by shore
bore nevermore

sea away say rain

o

now we ascend
a Fi Rebeacon Point
gravity pools
in my boots each
step up an event
each breath felt

point pools
each event
felt thought

SW108928
heading east

and thought
about as my
next breath's planned
shocked at nearly
sea-level moving
like an I used to

shocked sea like plod

plod at altitude
on alpine peaks
but I buckle
down to working

peaks buckle working here

up gradient here
now and be
gin enjoying
rhythm & mountain
memories of
movement

movement moment mum

for a moment
I'm my mum
on a Lakeland
fell's steep ridge
I see her eyes
frightened but
focused like

I frightened focused light

light between
clouds she is
meek & unsure
of mountains but will

not give in and
is vivid with glad
ness as long as
I stay close
and hold
her hand on
broken ground

glad as close hold on ground

steep slate steps
switchback

I look back down
to Nikki, her head's
down she's set in to
plodding steadily I
take her example I

will not stop
now to rest each
step banged out
in slow motion
each gasp a rope
of air pulled in
and coiled in me
to pull my soul
up on I love
this motion this
rhythm of flesh
& thought as sweat
wriggles out
of my skin to cool
a me by becoming
vaporous
as ghost
I'm nearing

motion rope in me

soul love this flesh

ghost nearing see

summit I can just see

a bench's wooden arm-rest
should I sit there or keep
a should moving
moving so I don't
get stuck still? another
step and more
another more emerges
bench emerges
and with it
a person so
it so that
that's answered that
I'll keep going I
straighten
my back quicken
my pace make
a relaxed & sprightly
mask for my
my my a mask tired
tired face
and give
an energised

hello to an elderly man

he returns
my word
his face
-skin sea
sea rip
rippling
pling sl
over slate
ate tee
bone teeming
ming soul
with soul
shine his green
eyes apple-round

and now a middle
aged-man with same
apple-eyes smiles as I
pass him on the path
he's dressed in
hi-tech fibres
designed to
wick sweat's
ghosts away
from his skin

same I path
in fibres
to sweat's away

and just behind him
apple-green repeated
in his teenage lad who
doesn't yet know what
his eyes do but sees

skin him
repeated who
what sees
his just him

same as his
two men just
ahead of him

o

Nikki takes
my hand now
not constrained
to single-
coastpath-file
we walk open
sloping fields

7km,
400m

suddenly in front of us rising
from coast-brow growing
with each step towards it

open fields rising
growing it

a black upthrust
of sheer wall
on tilted headland

SW110928

across bay a
Bucka Tor Cliff
hundreds of feet of
buckled slate back
dropping a church
-sized sea-stack
of an equal
ly black Gull Rock
and sprinkled

equal rock sprinkled
round arena miniaturised

on air round
this vast arena
/theatre miniaturised
by distance

swirling sharp-
white pin
point cries
of gulls glitter
-flakes shaken each
speck-bird a
tiny purpose in
chaos violently
white dots &
speed-swoop-streaks
laser-certain em
blazoned against
black slate another

distance-sharp pin cries glitter

white speed laser blazoned black

version of Kernow's
shadow/lit flag-colours

o

we pass on
turn in
land

Kernow's colours on in land

head south follow
paper's yellow-for-road to
wards a hamlet of a

Higher Bee Ny Tar
mac hard under
Vibram soles

sea is now unseen we

under soles we way-thorns

SW118925
heading easterly

duck into a hollow-way
arched over with thorns
and clogged
with keck & stingers
wind wipes leaves
above us but
in here air is still
and moist and laced
with insect flights
our skins itch
our throats are dry
we drink our bottle's
two last mouthfulls
my legs' muscles
feel hollow or full
of rushing space my
skeleton too heavy

still laced flights

my heavy emerge slopes

we emerge
onto gorzy slopes
Bee Ny stream
following its slot
below us

SW121925

stream slot us

Nikki gives
me her hazel
walking stick
I limp imagine

hazel stick imagine man-staff

an ancient man
& his wooden staff
struggling steadily
through mountainous desert

I pretend epic
pain to ease
pain

and now we discuss miles
& kilometres & convalescing &
pacing myself & intending

miles & intending

8km

a short walk & my
measuring which
should've been done
as I usually do
precisely with my
piece of trusty string but
an I only estimated
and judging by
our legs obviously
got wrong
badly but

measuring should as precisely piece I

suddenly I realise
an I knew all along
I'd wanted

realise along wanted distance

a distance
a distance

we've covered
today or revealed

I feel light's
changing heat as
sun's far fusion
seeps faint gold

changing sun's seeps

now we suck
through our noses
warm rich thick
honeysuckle scent
it's like sunlight felt
through our bodies
laughter's smell
and we're laughing
a me limping

thick scent felt

smell laughing limping

with a third leg
of hazel and
cracking
jokes about
Zimmer-frames
& mountains &
stairlifts &
sea-cliffs

cracking about frames

and her eyes beautiful
looking into me
light bounced
off unseen sea
is held in her
gaze & she's
here alive
& tired as I

beautiful me bounced

am
°

sea her she's alive I am
now cross ground

not far now
we cross
boggy ground
badly poached
by cattle

boggy badly by

we're surrounded
by tall prehistoric plants
like giant cow-keck
this is where a Bee
Ny stream springs
from to run some
two kilometres only
to plunge as a Pent
Argon Falls

be springs some only pent

somewhere around
SW127ish925ish

we step over
a thin string
of stream onto
firmer ground

onto ground over conducted rubs

an orchestra of
wind-conducted
grass-heads rubs
against our trousers
it's like wading
through dry liquid
waves breaking lit
seed-foam over
our boots

waves seed our now

now suddenly two huge sleek

conker-brown horses canter
towards us eager
to greet us

horses always cause
thoughts of my daughter
I remember a moment far
from sea in a Leicestershire
she's nine rides
horses' thoughts
through february light
I from she's through across
across glistening grass
gallops across paddock
hooves quickly repeat
moist thuds on
winter sward – warm
steam-plumes froth
from her pony's nostrils
ah, how well she rides
on february light!
light thuds scent
even though earth thuds
and there's soil's scent
it seems she's
learned to fly
from a far
she's fly-far sure heart
-side of field I'm sure
I hear her heart

huge horses
a mare & stallion
they seem to gleam
now standing flank
pressed to flank
muscles ocean-fluid
yet sculpted slate-solid
their rich brown pelts
ripple-twitching fly-itches

sheer wild force not
lost yet contained
-&-softened by
human husbandry

sheer lost & human

mole-pelt muzzles shiver
against our fingers
smooth warm breaths puff
like gentle hurricanes
into our palms

shiver fingers puff hurricane's palms

their sweat-scent
a slightly rude odour
of soily leathery oils
& pheromone haze

their eyes dark
polished globes
of deep & some
how liquid ground
holding glimpsed
horse-thoughts
fringed by thick
girl-curly lashes

some ground glimpsed

they are each a mass
of radiating animal energy
presences of health
their warmth oozes through
to my bones more sure
than hope and I

they of presences
their to than

could now
almost do
our whole
walk all over
again

(for one moment
in your life now
writer forget
poetry) there is

over again moment now
forget is other

no other

way of putting
it but these
horses these

these these

creatures

are simply glad
to meet us

imply ply

glad simply
to live ...

Step From I

side-step blood step step in time step
whiffs each step to step amongst about

to step steep slate-stepped key stepping
descending steps towards ascending steps

away & stepping over surf curl stepping
steps respects we step down we step from I

step wrong &nd

bolstered steps step-edge step across climb
steps each step steps I shout steps cross step

up an event steps switch back step banged
another step and more each step towards

step over

Mountain Mass, at Forty

for Austin

last night across Langstrath's valley
Pike o' Stickle purpled
under sky-sculpted light
cloud & ground thickened
into similar materials

gravity worked into mountain then

dark clarity & stars started
to sculpt water with zero's
fine crisp chiselling
ice skinned High House Tarn
put its crystal pattern
on tent fabric

we were like kids
giving our laughter to cold
with white breaths

we had left the men
of our sculptor & poet selves
somewhere below

        this morning the clocks turn
        so now is
        British Summer Time-&-ice

            across deep   Langstrath's shadow gap

            east's   sun thrusts at us

our tent fills with light
our water-bottles are solid
our faces warm & golden
Scafell Pikes polished
with silver snow

what a way to enter
one time from another

it's as if some god has given
us some secret about materials & souls
we shake our heads amazed
and smile as if filled with sky as

sunlight & mountain mass
bear our weights

Particular Winter, Trossachs, January 2010

late light crumbles
across Coire Earb

Cruach Ardrain fades
and crisps and fades
and cr

isps as

snow-smoke surges
on gusts' tuning

spindrift-twisters hiss
grains of glint-sting
on my cheeks like

radio taking my skin
I am granular light like
this gra nular-lit-ground
could I & land be blown

away on wind
as frozen smoke

? drift-ridges & ice-clad
grasses scatter
light's fast passing
of pale gold powders

a sheet

of solid lochan holds
shine tight on ice as
gauze -spooks of snow

sheeesh its gloss
a moment

of mountain hare fast
as a statue disintegrates
to white speed's

furry smoke -light

Now's Structures, Trossachs, January 2011

sun-wind-shine wip-sizzles soft   ly through fr   eezing air

my crampons cr   unk & chime on wind

-hardened snow-pack I'm   slung in winter's sky on

            a broad white ridge between

the snow-clothed Munros of   Beinn Glas & Ben Lawers

below Loch Tay's miles lay   as bluey-grey sky on

            snow's glossed-over lands

my crampons sh   ush-hiss through loose

gleaming snow-grains wind   lifts as smoke tr

            ails from my shins my

crampons creak on lay   ered works of wind

            wind   strea   mers of fro   zen sound   wind

layered snow-crystals cut   by motion into still   layered re

                        lief maps of   layering chaos organ

ised perfectly deep-   space-blue sky

            touches white

gleaming ground hung   a   bove snow-clean glens my

        crampons grip

crink and track slippery layers my finger   tips numb as glee's zeros

sculpt my want for for   ever as (s)now

Balance Sings

my feet feel

the roll
of a long
beech branch

air by &

below me
my hands green
with gravity

                                        light is

passing
through

my fingers
I sway
like a tree's

stillness
speeded
I stand

on a long
line of held
star-parts

          springy wood
          resounds with

the beautifully
weak force

of Earth's pull

only my feet
touch

my frame
sways free
arms divining
a star-heart's

vortex or

a deep pool
of time drying

I sway

feet planted
to bark as
roots topple
through soil's

unseen systems

I lift
a planted
foot rip
my position
and new

ly replace
a new shape

a beech stays

grace-filled

my feet feel
along a long
curved beech

limb this sway
as sweet

as saying

aremememberednameneverknownbefore

Pinnacle, Dinas Fach, Pembroke, April 2011

a prong of sea
-eroded rock-ground pokes

out into sea

from this horizontal spike a pinnacle rises

into sky here is a crossing

I cling

to a pinnacle ridge
ninety or more
feet below me sea hurls
curling cold whiteness onto

ground's edge

my son watches me

salted updraft scours
stone flecks of
ripped-off
lichen roil-&-flick
against my skin

sky wraps its fast fluids round
my small human form

o vertiginous sea-dream
on a pinnacle in wind
sea-swirl below o

o open ocean closing
in through noise

it has taken me my life's time to learn
to let ground
fall away either side of me and
for me

to sway-there-&-stay

nimble with this knowledgeless-involvement
I scamper back along the ridge to

my watching son

and then

a ground's -&- sky's -&- sea's moment

locks & opens
all at once

and again I'm on the pinnacle
but this time *with* my son

deadly distance compressed & pressing
in on the stone filament that together

we huddle on

and I cannot fathom his
young grace & sudden

skill his courage but

fine & still

as a stone edge between

surging sea & turbulant sky is

trust

Notes

Epigraph

'*The blue mountains are constantly walking...*' is taken from Gary Snyder's essay 'Blue Mountains Constantly Walking' (available in his 1990 essay collection *The Practice of the Wild*). Snyder receives these words from the 12th century Zen Buddhist monk, Dōgen Kigen; Kigen, in turn, is quoting from the 11th century Chan master Furong.

Lake, Needles, Thread & Paper

Take away the paper from your mouth is a Belgian saying, given to me by Ariane Thompson.

Lit Lichen, Tŷ Uchaf

Tŷ Uchaf is Welsh for *Upper House*. Petzl refers to a headtorch. (Petzl is the name of an outdoor equipment manufacturer that produces, amongst other things, headtorches.)

From a St Juliot to Beyond a Beeny

In August 2004 the River Valency (*Dowr an Velinji* in Cornish) flooded, causing extensive damage to the harbour village of Boscastle. It has been suggested that the name *Valency* is a corruption of the Cornish *Melinjy*, or *Melin-Chy*, which means mill-house, possibly referring to the mill in medieval times. The poem is full of 'corrupted' names. An extract from *From a St Juliot to Beyond a Beeny* was abstracted and reworked (or 're-mapped') for the Longbarrow Press anthology *The Footing* (2013).

Particular Winter, Trossachs, January 2010

Cruach Ardrain is a mountain near Crianlarich. Its name means *stack of the high part.*

Now's Structures, Trossachs, January 2011

Ben Lawers is one of the highest mountains in the Southern Highlands. Its name means *hill of the loud stream.* It is near to the village of Killin, at the head of Loch Tay.

Notes on *A*, *a*, *the*, *and* & *&*

To *And* or Amper's *&* (or not *per se*)

An author of this deploys a convention regarding the use of 'and' & '&'.

'&' is used like a buckle, to closely connect two things, ideas, feelings or events &c.. '&' gathers and brings together.

'And' is sometimes used as a story-esque-onwardsness, as in 'And so it happened ...' ... and 'and' is also placed to show moving from one action or location to another.

This convention's rule is sometimes broken, as in this case:

> fumbled & balanced

or in this case:

> & there are star-sharp need
> les & a thread

an author will leave further explanation and
leave it to a reader to create andswers

A bout A

Dear Ear,

Often my poetry about lANDscApe re()(f)uses the (or even a) definite article – a/the use of either 'A' or 'a' re(veals)inforces how land's cape is cons   tructed, is multiple & layered, and is only dist(rict)inct to 'a' person in 'a' moment, and that there is no de(a)f   inite interpretation of any layer, there is no 'the' person, 'the' moment, and especIally there is no 'the' poet, nor in()deed 'the' poem, or 'the' reader. I have (or some i has) one chapbook collection called *Distance a Sudden*, and a book called *Back of A Vast* ... the/a distinction(s) between lower & up   per case, and a/the difference in pronunciation of the/this/that first (thirst) letter of (y)our alpha bet, are all vital regarding meanings/ interpretations/cre@ions.

I (or an i) know that this/that/a my way of deploying a/the letter 'a' can jar, for some listener-readers – but that/this is as it is, and part of the/a poem's work, and an/the acceptance or rejection or tussle that a reader-maker (or breaker) experiences is to do with their relation   ship to the or a world made of (in)(out)(definite) art()icles   a reader can make a or not make a poem but 'the' poem cannot be made just as 'the' world is not 'The' yet is All words ...

Personal thanks

I am grateful to the following people, for critical comment and/or encouragement relating to individual poems or the entire manuscript: Elaine Aldred, Alan Baker, Allan Baker, Nick Bullock, Catherine Byron, Simon Cardy, Matthew Clegg, Arthur Crossland, Debs Davis, Jo Dacombe, Katie Daniels, David Devanny, Mark Gillies, Dr Mark Goodwin, Niall Grimes, Rob Hamberger, Neil Holland, Katie Ives, Helen Johnson, Chris Jones, Daithidh MacEochaidh, Michael Myshack, Austin Orwin, Tom Prentice, Gordon Stainforth, Mark Stevenson (aka Ghost Poet), Ariane Thompson, Pam Thompson, Michael Tolkien, Elaine Wheeler.

Thank you to Norman Jope & Jim Perrin for written appreciation of the manuscript.

Thank you to Julia Thornley for comments and encouragement regarding the form & content of *Steps*.

Thank you to James Wheeler for his knowledge of Amharic & its character font, his vital contribution to the Ethiopian poems in this collection, and especially for his closely connected & in-depth guiding whilst visiting him in Ethiopia in 2005.

Thank you to Brian Lewis for his precise yet open & creative style of editorship. *Steps* is very much a whole collaboration between creative editor & creative writer. The final intricate & meanings-laden layout of the whole book – from page-breaks to open field layout of certain poems, from contents page to pagination etc. – has depended on two creators encouraging and inspiring each other.

As ever, amazed gratitude to my partner Nikki Clayton for actually encouraging me & my commitment to making poetry, never mind putting up with it all! Above all though, thank you for making sure I kept taking steps when I could hardly walk ...